D1199428

the K concept

the K concept

We Are Always on Our Way
From Yesterday
Towards Tomorrow

Leif Klingborg

MAURITZ PUBLISHING

Beverly Hills, CA

© 2009 by Leif Klingborg

Mauritz Publishing
269 S. Beverly Dr. #1065
Beverly Hills, CA 90212
Phone: 310-745-8400

All rights reserved. No part of this book may be reproduced, stored in a retrieval system or transmitted in any form or by any means—electronic or mechanical, photocopy, recording, or any other—except for brief quotations in printed reviews, without the prior permission of the publisher.

This publication is designed to provide accurate and authoritative information in regard to the subject matter covered. It is sold with the understanding that neither the authors nor the publisher are engaged in rendering legal, accounting, or other professional service or advice.

Second printing.

Printed in China.

Publisher's Cataloguing-in-Publication

Klingborg, Leif.

The K concept / Leif Klingborg. -- Beverly Hills, CA : Mauritz Pub., c2009.

p. ; cm.

ISBN: 978-0-9841021-7-4
Subtitle on cover: We are always on our way from yesterday towards tomorrow.

1. Leadership. 2. Motivation (Psychology) 3. Development leadership. 4. Executive coaching. 5. Success in business I. Title.

HD57.7 .K55 2009   2009931609
658.4/092--dc22   0910

Book Consultant: Ellen Reid
Jacket Design: Chris Collins
Cover Photograph and Author Photograph: Joakim Bergstrom
Interior Design and Layout: Ghislain Viau
Editing: Pamela Guerrieri

Life is a step-by-step learning development process!

*I dedicate this book to my parents, teachers, leaders,
coaches, and all who inspired me.*

With this book, my hope is to inspire you!

Contents

Introduction

The K Concept is the core in my support to you as you develop your business.

My overall goal is to bring you as the leader, your team, and your company, closer to the edge of your market.

You have the opportunity to strengthen your business through building a more development-oriented process towards "who you want to be."

The K Concept will support you in finding "the best way" in your business.

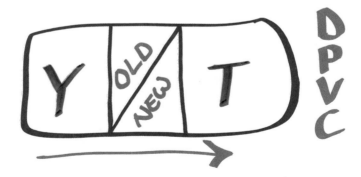

I like to describe the development we are part of with this picture, telling us:

We are always on our way, from yesterday towards tomorrow, somewhere between the old and the new. This is our direction.

Our role as leaders is to connect our co-workers' hearts and minds in "the mental creation" of our future opportunities and then support them step-by-step to move there.

In every company and organization we will establish this movement through:

D – Making choices about our common Direction.

P – Building supportive Pictures of how to accomplish our movement in a well-organized way.

V – Discussing Values important for building a solid progress.

C – Identifying and developing the unique Competencies that will take us towards the edge.

The CEO or the president of the company is the overall process owner, responsible for this development in each part of the business.

The K Concept will support leaders in mobilizing their co-workers to be the driving force in this development.

Leadership is our most powerful resource when creating our world of tomorrow.

We can all grow in our leadership roles of guiding people and processes to a successful future.

This book will empower your thinking process about how to create your tomorrow, showing how important you are as the leader bringing along your unique part.

This book will give ideas, inspiration, and tools for how you can support individuals and teams to upgrade their thinking processes, releasing their ambition into their proactive constructive development.

In discussions with leaders over the years, regarding how they can further develop themselves to lead, or take opportunities to grow towards executive positions, we have found suggestions like:

1. Find the best mentor.

2. Build yourself strong in your current role so you can choose the interesting job process that will take you forward.

3. Find and connect yourself with networks that give you what you are really looking for.

4. Build up your own network, the core of people with whom you can make a difference.

5. And always remember, it is about them! It's about the people connected to your process and their development. It's about how you can get them to generate energy, intelligence, skills, and tactics.

This book will touch all five areas, providing you with understanding and tools, how to speed up your co-workers' development, building further on their unique skills, personalities, ambitions, and expectations.

In order to help you get to know me better, I want to highlight some of my own development with connection to these five areas:

1. Find the best mentor.

I met the legendary business consultant Mike Kami on a top leadership forum. He was the experienced man from whom I could get confirmation regarding all of the development processes inside our supported companies that now were rapidly growing.

Mike shared his deep understanding and highlighted the accelerating technological development, stressing how we as human beings have lots of work to do to adapt to upcoming opportunities.

He found the K Concept, and how my consultants and I were supporting our customers, very interesting. His sharp feedback and constructive support gave us broader perspectives. He gave us the key words "understanding development" to describe what we were doing.

By the way, Mike still thinks I can be a better listener and that I want to do too much at once, and I know he is right.

2. Build yourself strong in your current role, so you can choose your further development.

I had been growing in my role as consultant, and now I was chosen in hard competition to support ABB—a worldwide engineering company and leader in power and automation technologies.

ABB took my help to develop a leadership program with the K Concept as the core. At the same time we were building up a master plant where they all started to train and work following the concept. Both became success stories; I was part of an "interesting process."

The strong leader behind the development in ABB was the CEO Percy Barnevik. He was voted as the number one CEO and ABB as the number one company in Europe by 500 top leaders. The movement inspired people to develop themselves, their working processes, and their companies into something extraordinary.

Barnevik had a formula for creating development through building a decentralized organization.

The challenges, responsibility, and trust I received over the years from the ABB people helped me to grow a lot.

3. Find the networks that give what you are really looking for.

I attended top management forums in Europe and the U.S. looking for upgrading and connections. I learned a lot about the bigger picture from business leaders, other consultants, and when global leading politicians gave their explanations.

Other conferences were more about understanding myself. Leading consultants and business leaders shared more personal situations and experiences with the perspective of challenging working situations, looking for balance in life.

I've been involved in sports since I was a kid. I was a top-level player, and I was a successful coach. Today my network of top sport leaders and people in the Federation is keeping me engaged with the feeling of still being valuable and connected.

4. Build up your own network of people with whom you can make a difference.

I have constantly worked to secure the strongest network of people committed to accelerating the movement in each organization we support. People with determination to move forward, to connect, involve, decide, and deliver, helping from the outside the various ambitions inside the organizations. As leaders, we are coordinating our forces to give the best support, building on each person's complementary strengths.

I am grateful to have had the opportunity of working with lots of people filled with big ambitions, in business life as well as in the world of sports.

5. It's all about them! Your team! Grow your team and you will grow as leader.

This book is built on interrelated blocks, supporting you to build up your own strategy and drive to be the successful leader, coach, or mentor who takes people towards their dreams.

Each block will first give you ideas and inspiration to your overall thinking process. The last part of each block will challenge you to bring along your team and other stakeholders. Together with your team, you will find out about new approaches to win respect in the marketplace.

You will grow in your role because of your determination to provide your people with an environment of progress and learning how to generate and give value in various practical situations.

Your leadership, together with your team, will develop something unique, untouchable, winning. And my role is to support you.

I want to be your guide, your coach. I will call myself your mentor throughout this book.

Before going into the blocks, here is some more guidance …

I want your mindset to be new and fresh! So tell yourself:

I have great knowledge, experiences, and insights. This is my starting point! I am always a part of something bigger, and I will develop myself in this bigger context. My pro-activity will take me into new interesting situations. I will find myself in a new light.

As mentor I want to give you this!

Use this book as a "training myself support."

Read one block at a time. Take notes to connect to what you are already doing. Do your special task. Communicate with your selected key people. Make your choices. Do your training and preparation and try it out with your team.

Make sure to listen carefully to the selected key people in your organization, the people who were and are building your bridges. This openness will bring you closer to well-grounded choices, which give you the best motivation to train and develop yourself to act more efficient.

You will upgrade, chapter by chapter, ensuring your progress.

Draw and write a lot! This will release your potential.

A big goal for me as your mentor is to inspire you to draw and write like I did on the initial page, in order to really connect to the source of options and potential you have inside.

This drawing and writing concept will take you into a winning position. Most of what we are looking for we have the answer to, inside ourselves.

Your images and writings connect and release; it will free your creativity, it will ask you for simple priorities. Both will help your conscious and subconscious work for you.

I will share my hand-drawn images and handwriting to convince you about the genuine power of having your own basic handmade pictures guiding your movement. Other situations will demand the latest technological support. You will handle both.

Trying it out chapter-by-chapter will guarantee your progress.

Final Input:

I will communicate with you from different perspectives, jumping between you, we, and I as I just did.

I will use the word *leadership* for what this is all about and the people on your team are your co-workers.

Growing clarity on how you can really make a difference in leading your unique part tells how the blocks are valuable for you.

It's all about "who you want to be" and your important contributions when connecting and developing individuals and teams towards their ambitions and their dreams about "who they want to be."

Most Importantly ...

Fill in the picture on the next page with the most important actions that you see for your company and team moving forward.

Your picture will guide and direct your thinking process towards fruitful ways of acting.

The better you know what you really want to achieve, the better the outcome of your thinking processes.

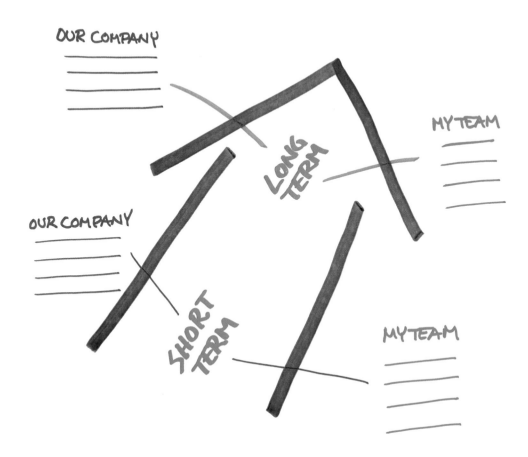

OUR COMPANY

MY TEAM

LONG TERM

OUR COMPANY

SHORT TERM

MY TEAM

KEY WORDS GUIDING MY GROWTH THROUGH THIS BOOK
PLEASE ADD 4 MOST IMPORTANT ACTIONS EACH PART

Part One

Building the Strong, Safe, and Secure Team

OUR PROCESS

WHEN WE GIVE OUR THOUGHTS MORE DIRECTION
WE WILL BE MORE INTERESTED IN HOW TO GET THERE

1

Our Process!

The process of taking our team and our company towards our ambitions has a dimension of beauty.

The following input will support your overall thinking about a development process.

Read it 2–3 times. Take notes to establish a deeper connection to your current insights and extract what you want to bring to your team's movement.

The Dream

- I had a dream about running a marathon.
- I envisioned all of the runners, the crowd lining the street, musicians, flags …
- I wanted to be a part of the whole big party.

Is it Realistic?

One day I saw information advertising the Chicago Marathon.

I thought, *This is it!* I wanted to take part in the event. But then I wondered, *Is it realistic?*

The race was 40 kilometers, and I only had four months to prepare.

I analyzed my situation using the following assessment:

1. Today I am able to run 10 kilometers.
2. I can increase to 20 kilometers by the end of the second month.
3. I will be able to add another 2.5 kilometers every week, which will take me to 30 kilometers by the end of the third month.

Suddenly I realized, *Wow, I can do it! I can walk the last part. It's challenging, but it's realistic.*

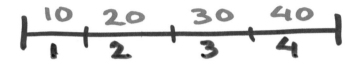

When we understand that something can be done, we can fulfill our dream. We want to make our choice to go for it!

Making My Choice

Making my choice, I had learned to:

1. See myself reaching my goal; imagine myself being there, my feelings.
2. Look over my shoulder and face all of the work required to achieve my goal.
3. Ask myself, *Do I really want to do this?*
        When the answer is yes, I make my choice.

Establishing My Vision

Another way to describe what is happening when we decide to go for something is to say that we are "establishing a vision."

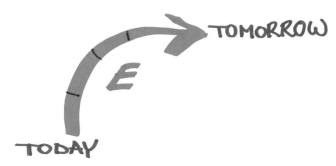

There is something we are not able to do today that we want to be able to do tomorrow. The structural tension between who we are today and who we want to become will release energy into our development. When we have a big vision that requires a large amount of work, we break it down into smaller steps with partial goals.

For me to reach my goal of running the Chicago Marathon, I already had my partial steps laid out. Soon, I was out running. I met people who had previously run the marathon and I voiced lots of questions …

There Is a lot of Support

I remember meeting one man who told me there is a magazine with all of the information and guidance you will need to prepare for the marathon. You can find it in the store next to where you live.

This is how it is. We have access to lots of important information and supportive people are surrounding us when we know what we want to do and who we want to be.

The Steps

I learned a lot about outfits, training, and nutrition, and I felt proud when I summarized my first step. Realizing what I had accomplished in the first step gave me even more momentum when moving into the second step.

Sometimes I was training in the morning, sometimes at lunchtime, and sometimes in the evening. I was energized, and my choice had opened me up to think and act in new and interesting ways. Eventually, I started spinning and experimenting with other kinds of workouts. I made new friends and we shared our ambitions and had fun together.

I felt even prouder when evaluating my second step, where I had added to the amount of training and learned more about the preparation for running my marathon. I recognized that I had a new perception about my whole journey. Before the challenge, we think we have everything figured out and know how it will be. In the middle of my preparations for the race, my experience grew and matured into a new dimension. I realized that I was a runner and I felt ownership.

Learning Development

The day I made my choice was the birth of the vision. The day I ran the marathon was the fulfillment.

Between birth and fulfillment, there is a time frame. The time frame can be long or short, depending on how ambitious the vision is and how much effort and time I am willing to put into reaching fulfillment.

This process is about training and challenging work in order to assimilate, to accommodate, and to grow into being a marathon runner.

This is the process for everything regardless of our ambitions, from learning how to golf to developing language skills, and this is the way it is for our teams and their ambitions.

The beauty is that we all know a lot about this. First we walk, then we run, then we jump.

Life is a step-by-step learning-development process. Each step takes time—for practice and progress.

The more we are able to see and connect with each other, the more we will be able to help each other take our following step.

This process is obvious to see with our small children. We really want to connect, to be their role model, and, for example, teach them how to walk. We want to emotionally connect to the children, releasing a positive energy around the learning situation: "Yes, great! You can do it!" The positive climate will open us up to give, to receive, and to move forward.

Accelerating Our Teams

You and I as leaders know so much about all this. We are working hard to accelerate our team's learning development process to capture the opportunities in the market. We want to connect every co-worker into our vision and into our choices so they all will be able to release their energy and grow their potentials.

However, their motives will be different and they will contribute in unique ways. We are all complementary.

Since we are united in our vision, we will find out about our common unique steps.

After several steps, we will approach the "step of option."

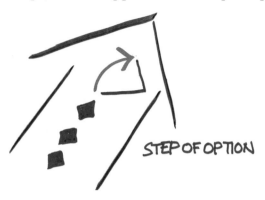

STEP OF OPTION

We will reach the "step of option" because we have been generating:

- Strategic intelligence
- Skills
- Insights
- Self-confidence to find out about our own unique way

From the "step of option," we will see new products and new services launched in the market and we will watch athletes and sports teams taking their sports into new dimensions.

This is where I want to take my team so we can differentiate ourselves and contribute to the successful future of our company, our team, and ourselves.

Now it is time for your reflections about the process.
- *Write your four most important insights on the following page.*
- *Draw and write your picture of the development that will take you and your team towards your ambition; take support of what you just read.*

VALUABLE INSIGHTS – 4 MOST IMPORTANT

_____

_____

_____

_____

THE PROCESS TOWARDS OUR AMBITION

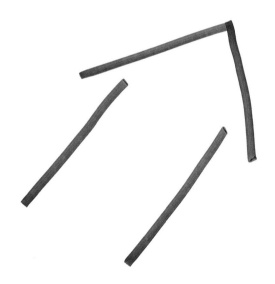

CONTINUE TO DRAW AND WRITE YOUR DEVELOPMENT

Moving towards your ambition

You now have your picture about the development that will take your team towards your ambitions! Imagine building up this picture with your whole team involved. Imagine building up this picture so short-term and long-term ambitions will be in line, adding on to give the best clarity and motivation. That is the K Concept!

Your choice to grow your co-workers' ownership of their development will accelerate your movement. You will develop a more holistic approach, a structured and well-organized way of acting together. You will end up with the intelligent company.

To really involve your people in building your company of tomorrow, the first part of the K Concept will support you to build a strong, safe, and secure process by using the first four basic blocks: Gather the team, Co-worker in the center, We spirit, and Documentation.

The second part of the K Concept will be to accelerate out of that platform, building the intelligent company step-by-step.

The third part of this book guides us to understand how important we are as leaders when leading towards tomorrow.

The final part is to polish our unique core as leaders and reflect on how we want to connect ourselves to further important roles on our amazing journey in life.

As mentor I used to reflect on …

How we give releasing contributions to what we all love deep inside: Development. This is easy to understand through the happiness we feel as parents or friends meeting, a first smile, word, step, friend, reading, graduation, great performance ...

Development is so emotional and wonderful; we are all part in the big development happening right now, and tomorrow.

Our Process!

GATHERTHETEAM

UNDERSTANDING AND PARTICIPATION WILL CONNECT MY CO-WORKER'S AMBITIONS INTO OUR OPPORTUNITIES

2

Gather the Team

G_ather the team_ is the first block to build a strong, safe, and secure development process.

This is where our team's common thinking process starts, refreshes, and accelerates.

The following input will now help stimulate your thinking process about gathering your team:

- Read it 2–3 times.
- Take notes to evoke your own clarity.
  Extract parts you want to bring to your team.

I am the leader—this is my team.
I want us to be a high-performance team.

My Role

Establishing our cooperation, I am asking my co-workers questions of importance, like:

1. How do you want to be seen? Their answers can range from:
   As important
   With competence
   Highly motivated to do a great job

2. What is important for me in my role as your leader then? They may say:
   To create understanding of, and involvement in, our working process.

3. How do we reach the edge then? What's behind winning? Their ideas may be:
   We will develop the best common ground so it will be easy for us to cooperate efficiently inside our team. We will then develop skills and build up relationships to create value with people outside our team.

Lots of Ambitions

We have lots of ambitions inside our teams. Our role as leaders is to connect every co-worker with the opportunities out there in the market.

The market is always new!

I know that my co-workers are expecting me to lead the development of our perspectives, so we will be able to keep up our constructive mindset, where the market is our source of energy, and the pull we need it to be.

I know that my co-workers are expecting me to take responsibility, so we will have the best supportive pictures and road maps for doing an excellent job or to develop our unique creation.

Our New Track

Taking ownership of my process, I will take my team off the old track to do some thinking and discussion.

We will look back and analyze yesterday; we want to look forward to do some sketching about tomorrow.

Looking back, all my co-workers have experiences and insights. It is essential to extract and bring with us the factors that took us to success in the past, to understand our core and our soul.

Looking forward, all my co-workers have dreams and expectations. They just love to be involved in creating and painting the picture of tomorrow, deciding or refreshing who we want to be in certain time frames.

Our discussion will soon come down to the important questions we have today, in our search for clarity in how to move forward.

Give Ownership

I will inspire my co-workers by posing these questions to my team. I will encourage everyone to think through, discuss, and write down their best ideas to move every important question forward.

This is the core of "gathering the team." We support each other to:

- See more
- Understand more
- Organize information
- Lift important questions
- Paint the unique picture of our value stream

I will collect input from everyone, and we will soon have this on our flip chart:

- The smartest ideas we have inside our team
- What we feel is right

You and I as leaders know that when we are opening up our co-workers' hearts and minds, we are bringing them to the point of decision-making.

We will soon be able to make our choice. We do like this!

A Business Is Spelled "We"

This is the best that I can give to all my co-workers so they can be extremely professional when meeting people from outside our team.

Meeting a customer, my co-worker can say:

- Looking back we can see this.
- Looking forward we want to be this.
- Today this represents our best ideas, and this is what we feel is right, so now we want to establish this win-win situation together with you.

We Are Generating Momentum

My role as leader is to make everyone on my team successful. When my co-worker offers valuable input to our customers, she will receive positive vibes back. When I ask her about this, she will say:

It feels good receiving pluses; it gives me confidence.

Then she will say:

- It brings in money
- It generates valuable information
- It will make our customers speak well about us

Listening to her I will think, "This is great!"

I know that even better will be the fact that she will soon realize and appreciate the market-driven learning development process we have been establishing inside our team.

Our more efficient way of cooperating will really motivate her and all my co-workers to:

- Bring in the best knowledge there is in our niche
- Develop desire for engaging in important discussions

Together, we will now be able to make our essential choices, the choices that will step-by-step create our movement.

Your reflection!

- Please write your four most valuable insights about gathering your team towards your ambitions.

- Then continue into the "gather the team" training.

VALUABLE INSIGHTS - GATHER THE TEAM

1
2
3
4

THE FOLLOWING PAGES WILL SUPPORT YOU IN PROVIDING YOUR TEAM WITH THREE BASIC COMMON PICTURES

FOLLOW THE SCRIPT - YOU WILL TRAIN

Broad common pictures are the foundation for the common thinking process in your team.

Gather your team. First you always do the social part—connecting everyone on an easy recreational question. Once connected, you move on.

Let everyone draw three pictures of your company, one of Yesterday, one of Today, and one of Tomorrow. Make them simple pictures. Give 4–5 minutes for preparation.

Give everyone 1–2 minutes to present his or her view, inspire open minds, give everyone the same amount of time and attention. Ask the teammates to take notes from each other's presentations.

When finished, ask the team to please write down their reflections after listening to each other, first about yesterday. Then take one input from each co-worker, and write the contribution on the flip chart. When you have all inputs, simply repeat them all, saying, "This is what we said …"

You ask if this broader picture is okay, and maybe you or the team will add something, but your ambition is to move on.

Now you ask your team to write down their reflections about tomorrow … Take one input from each co-worker, write it on the flip chart, and then just repeat.

Lastly you ask the team—with this clarity about yesterday and the direction about tomorrow—what do we find as most important for us to act on today?

Our common broader pictures give us context for further cooperation.

Building our common pictures, we follow this formula:

It starts with individual preparation around the question at hand, then listen to each other, take notes, and then reflect. Working like this we support our team to develop common insights; it will give clarity, direction, and agreement. It will strengthen belonging and identity.

Of course, we have done this one way or another. The key is to regularly polish our guiding pictures. The key is to develop our skills to provide our team with the best supporting pictures.

Connecting Your Co-workers Towards the Market Edge

Draw this picture of your company on the flip chart. Tell your co-workers: this is the lead team, this is "we," and these are other teams.

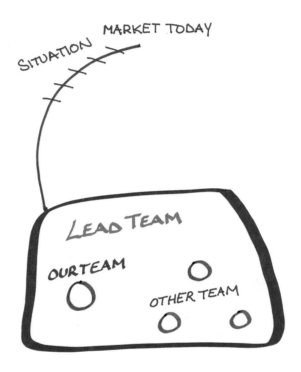

Then you start to build your common picture, asking: How is the situation in the market today?

Your co-workers will write down their input, then you collect one from each. You write down their inputs on the flip chart; after they all have given their ideas, you read through them, beginning with, "This is our view of the market today ..."

Next, you ask if it covers their broader view, and they will say "okay" or they might add something.

Then you ask: "So what do we and other companies do to be a strong player out there?" They write down their ideas. You collect one input from each at a time, with the option to take additional laps.

Then you read out loud all of what you have written on the flip chart. If needed, add additional comments.

Let your team know how great it is that you are united into this common view.

Next, tell your co-workers to be the strong team, building ourselves a great tomorrow. We of course want to look into the future 2–3 years ahead from now. You ask them to write down their ideas of how the situation in the market will be. You collect and read through, maybe adding …

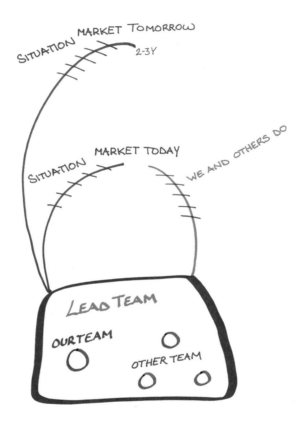

As your picture is growing within the team, you ask: What will we and other companies do to be out there in the market in the future? Your co-workers will write down their ideas, and maybe you ask them to discuss two and two. Then you ask them to be united about their most important inputs. You collect one input from each pair; maybe you take a second lap. Then you repeat …

You ask the team what to name these last inputs. They will say it's a kind of vision. When you ask them how it feels, they will probably say that it's crucial to be united, and the common direction will make it easier to cooperate and you will smile …

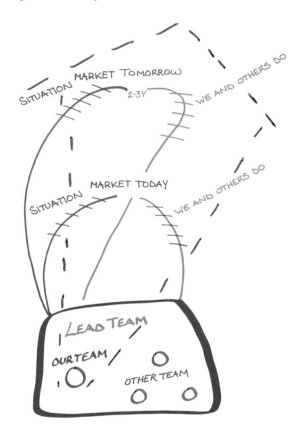

The team's common pictures will build up self-confidence within the team and into each member. Your role as leader is to support your team to first come up with their thoughts; this will give them strength to open up … Now, they will be interested in and understand more of the executive team's business strategies and what is going on in other teams inside and outside their company.

Establishing Our Team

Working with my team, I am responsible for bringing clarity to support efficient internal cooperation, so together with my team we will:

- Decide how we want to be recognized as a team from our stakeholders' perspectives.
- Clarify expectations we have of each other when cooperating towards our ambition

First I will ask my team:

Who do we want to be?
How do we want to be recognized?

They write down …

I collect …
I repeat …
We agree …

Thereafter, I will ask my team, now moving forward with ambition, to be what we have decided to be.

What is your expectation of me as your leader?

Next I ask, trying to be what we have decided, and considering your expectations of me:

What can I expect from you?

I will discuss with my team how we can save this flip chart, so every now and then during our process we can reflect back on our ambitions and expectations.

We can rate how we are doing.
We can see what works out well.
We can see where to put more energy behind our efforts.
We can see what we may want to exclude or add.

Holding on to our document's guidance will give us success.

We find that we have much inside, of both questions and answers, when we get connected into a well-organized development process, helping each other out as a team.

Having clarity about our team's most essential pictures will give space for our next most important.

Your reflection!

- Please fill in the template on the following page with the sharp thoughts you now have in mind about creating key pictures.

CRUCIAL WHEN BUILDING UP - YOUR PICTURES

NOW WE HAVE SPACE FOR NEXT LEVEL OF
IMPORTANT GUIDING PICTURES

FIND AND BUILD THESE PICTURES WITH YOUR TEAM

Co-worker in the Center

FOR VARIOUS REASONS WE JUST LOVE AND NEED
TO SIT DOWN WITH OUR LEADER TO BRING CLARITY
ABOUT OUR BEST CONTRIBUTIONS

3

Co-worker in the Center

Co-worker in the center is the second block in building a strong, safe, and secure development.

This is where we create the platform from which our individual co-worker can grow.

Read the input 2–3 times. Take notes and extract your parts.

My Role

You and I, as leaders, know that every co-worker needs the best individual relationship with their leader to be able to release their full potential.

I will sit down with each one of my co-workers and put them in the center.

My ambition with our dialogue is to support everyone to:

- Be more self-dependent
- Take more initiatives
- Take on more responsibility
- Extend their desire to learn

During our "gather the team" session, we have been upgrading pictures of the Value Stream, Company, and Team. We have been through discussions about who we want to be, and the best way for us to move in that direction.

In every gather the team discussion, I have been encouraging all my co-workers to write down their best and most valuable contribution, as well as what can be crucial for supporting their teammates to develop and reach mutual success with our customers.

Crucial to Talk About …

Next, I will meet with each of my co-workers so we can go through everything we have gathered in our process so far. We will be analyzing, brainstorming with the overall goal to support each other with the best individual picture. To fully prepare for this meeting I will ask my team:

"From your current point of view, which questions do you find most important to cover during our co-worker in the center meeting?"

Each one will write down their ideas, I will collect input from everyone, and we will soon have an extremely supportive common document to strengthen both parties' preparation.

Our Meeting

Now it's time to sit down, and I will listen carefully. All my co-workers have vital and necessary information for me about customers, our team, and other teams.

I will learn a lot, and during our dialogue we will find areas that they know more about and areas where I can add further information. We can discuss how to bring in support and inputs from outside sources, and find out methods to train and develop crucial skills.

I will stimulate every co-worker to be extremely active and participative, to draw and write, and I will ask supportive and specific questions in order to fully upgrade understanding and involvement.

The Core

This is the core of the co-worker in the center—when we together are creating pictures, scenarios, evaluating situations, information, examining our business strategy, and so on.

The key for us is to find out how to move forward, together. It is a lot about identity, meaningfulness, energy, and mutual respect for our roles.

This is the way I support my co-workers to grow with our movement, reflecting on their contributions in the past and how they will be valuable from different perspectives in the future.

I will develop unique insights about how their individual experiences, knowledge, skills, and desires are complementary to each other, and about how we can take full advantage of that as a team.

They Are All My Co-workers

Meeting with my co-workers, I will find out and learn about their unique personal approaches:

- Some are more individually driven
- Others are like the oil in the machinery
- Some want to carry the group's vision
- Others want to stand a little bit behind with more external objectivity

Still, they are all my co-workers and together we can be something special.

Down the road our guiding keyword will be "edge in our market."

Goals and Plans

When building up a great team, it's essential that what the co-workers want to be is fully in line with what our company wants to be in the market.

This will motivate us to connect into our common goals and plans.

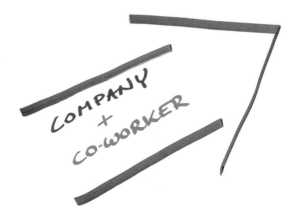

I know that my co-workers regularly want us to upgrade pictures, goals, and plans. They often say:

"The broader and deeper pictures we have, the better we can feel the pull from the market. The clearer we can see our roles, the more value we are able to put into our working process."

Then they say:

"This fresh picture will be extremely supportive to you as our leader, so you can give the best daily and weekly feedback and support to all of us, your co-workers."

Your reflection!

– Please fill the template on the following page with what's most important when growing your co-workers towards your team's ambition.
– Find out how to do your training to open up your co-workers for proactive discussions.
– List your co-workers' strengths, think through their opportunities to grow and how you will establish the best interaction to support growth.

FOUR MOST IMPORTANT INSIGHTS

1
2
3
4

TRAINING MYSELF TO OPEN UP MY CO-WORKERS

WHAT IS
FUN _____ _____ _____

WHAT ARE YOU
GOOD AT _____ _____ _____

WHAT DO YOU
WANT TO DEVELOP _____ _____ _____

WHAT IS YOUR
CONCERN _____ _____ _____

- ASK EACH QUESTION - WRITE DOWN KEY-WORDS FROM THE ANSWER
- WHEN THROUGH ALL QUESTIONS - REPEAT - ADD DISCUSS..
- HAND OVER PAPER
- GO FURTHER INTO MOST IMPORTANT FOR BOTH OF YOU

LIST ALL YOUR Co-WORKERS

NAME	THEIR STRENGTHS	THEIR DEV. OPTIONS	YOUR APPROACH

Co-worker in the Center

THE WE SPIRIT

WE

AN ORGANIZATION IS SPELLED WE AND
WE ARE GENERATING PROACTIVITY TOGETHER
WITH OTHER PEOPLE

4

The We Spirit

The *We Spirit* block will support your thinking about how your co-workers are developing cohesion and establishing the emotional drive, the spirit towards your ambition.

Read the input 2–3 times. Take notes to generate ideas. Extract essentials to bring to your team.

Cohesion

As leaders, we recognize a deep satisfaction when we have been creating a strong spirit inside our teams so we can feel stability and have courage to meet every situation ahead of us.

We create the we spirit by listening carefully to our co-workers. Their goals and expectations are often in the realm of building stronger cohesion.

Releasing Energy

The we spirit is connected to our energy centers and our basic human needs. We know that most of our co-workers' needs will be fulfilled in their working situation, supported by the company culture.

They are involved in numerous activities, stretching all the way to broader, more organized, social, physical, and cultural events. The connection between our co-workers will be deeper and stronger when they have the opportunity to see and meet each other in new, slightly different situations.

This will create openness and release their energy.

Our Role as Leaders

One important factor of the we spirit is the way we behave as leaders. The old style of leadership was more about commanding or throwing single questions at the team. We know today that this may cause defensive behavior or a polarization between strong individuals. To better cope with the developments in the market, we are looking for new and innovative ways to lead our people, working more out of frames or with directions, expecting every co-worker to deliver their best ideas to every important question within our team.

This method of first gathering everyone on a more social and emotional level will create a foundation to comfortably support each other on the intellectual level during our growing cooperation. Developing trust through social connection is crucial when co-workers are asked to deliver unique contributions in a challenging market situation.

The ancient Greeks showed us that ethos and pathos are door openers for establishing logical thinking processes.

What Is Going on Outside the Team?

Strong spirit inside our team will soon lead to growing interest about what is going on outside of the team environment. This will give me, as the leader, great opportunities to support my co-workers to see and learn about other important individuals and teams. My team and I will learn about their:

- Expectations
- Goals
- Training
- Strategies

With open minds, we can learn a lot about the possibilities in our business.

Our common insights will make us stronger in our choices on how to support each other to take initiatives when meeting important people and teams.

With knowledge about and connections in the market, we can now support each other to engage in a more proactive approach. We give, in hope of receiving when we connect with strategically chosen partners, establishing crucial win-win scenarios. We make sure to have all the pieces of our pie fully thought through with our teammates before meeting our business friends, and we help each other out during our initiatives and analysis.

We will grow our mutual understanding that our customer is looking for certain value, and we help each other understand how this will affect our future value. We want to bring clarity to how every business relation will affect our overall strategic development.

Our Mindset

Openness and high energy are keys to learning and development. I know that my co-workers' minds are following certain tracks, and I want them to upgrade.

I know that they are upgrading when they take influences from other individuals or teams, either directly—through interaction—or indirectly by reading or watching their inputs using any kind of media.

We are receiving our influences from other people.

When my co-workers start to see each other and other individuals and teams as resources to their own development, I know we have the right mindset for success.

Your reflections!

- Secure your thoughts about taking your team towards your ambition.

- Recognize and list various we spirit qualities that you see in each player on your team.

- Fill the template about crucial connections, and how you will grow together towards your ambition.

VALUABLE TO BRING TO MY TEAM

1
2
3
4

KEY PEOPLE IN MY TEAM FROM DIFFERENT
WE - PERSPECTIVES

_____
_____
_____
_____

WE

KEY CONNECTIONS FOR THE SUCCESS
OF MY TEAM AND ME AS LEADER (IND AND TEAMS)

NAME	THEIR STRENGTHS	OUR WIN-WIN	OUR COMMON DEV.

DOCUMENTATION

TOGETHER WITH MY TEAM I CREATE THE OUTSIDE-IN
PERSPECTIVE WE NEED TO GROW IN A WELL ORGANIZED
WAY

5

Documentation

Our ***Documentation*** will support our team to build up the intellectual overview to take the lead in our field.

Read the input 2–3 times. Take notes of interest. Extract the parts you want to bring to your team.

Our Document

Supporting our movement towards the edge of the market, the block of documentation will build up our team's ability to read and understand different situations and stages in our development.

Our co-workers' view is that the market is rapidly renewing and they want to feel ownership of their situation.

We can easily support the team to create a document that reflects our co-workers' view of their broader working situation as well as their own roles.

We Do it Ourselves

The goal is to grow each co-worker's awareness about what is going on in their business, and to reflect their own roles in the perspective of our development towards our company's strategy.

A couple of our co-workers can easily take photos and ask questions, use a video camera, or create a meeting place on the Web. The purpose is to connect people into what's going on, they will all be visualized, and every team member will have the opportunity to give their view.

Some of our co-workers may express their views about the past period of work, such as successes, important relationships, and special activities. Other co-workers may give their views on the present; e.g., about our market situation, our strengths, and what they think we need to develop. Some can look into our next period and give input about their expectations and predictions about the market, work, and relationships. Still others can give their views about our long-term opportunities.

Important Information

In our documentation we can further convert information from the top to be more specific and understandable. We can highlight customers and suppliers, and reflect on how we are building up our value stream in cooperation with them. We can show successful external individuals and teams in order to learn from them.

Working in this more holistic perspective will build up our co-workers' self-confidence. They will be stronger when they start to reflect on what they have been doing, what they have been doing well, and what they are particularly good at. They will be stronger the more united they are around what is most important in the short term, and when they understand how this fits into what is most important in the long term.

This is how we are connecting our co-workers into our movement. Growing their confidence will accelerate their interest in what's going on out there in the market and in the guidelines established from the top.

We Develop Ownership of Our Own Development

We support our co-workers to grow their vision side as well as their analytical side. They need figures; they want statistics. They want to measure, compare, and understand how to develop their strategic intelligence and skills with the ambition to raise their international competitiveness and adaptability into new value streams. New keywords will be workflow, standards, logistics, modules, and new ways to communicate.

The market is rapidly developing. Our determined work has put us in a position where we feel growing ownership about our working situation, with the ambition to take the lead.

This is the kind of process we all want to be involved in and our role as leaders is to build on our co-workers' constructive, proactive, creative ideas.

Reflecting our progress in our own documentation will give lots of excitement to each team member. We all want to review our documentation together with teammates, but also with friends and family. The review gives us a fresh perspective about our own situation, our team, and our future.

The documentation will support us with the external objectivity we need to take the lead.

We Develop a Process-Oriented Mindset

As a leader I will use our documentation to support my team in looking from outside in, to raise our awareness of how to work in a more process-oriented well-organized way. In the first review meeting I will highlight when we started up our first step, our first project, our first process … We didn't have much of a picture. We only had some information from the top and we were listening to each other, to customers, suppliers, and looking at other successful teams.

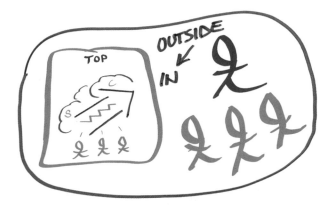

It was a lot of testing, training, learning, and struggling before we could deliver.

Now when we are going to take our next step, I will ask my team what will be crucial for success. Their ideas may be to create the best common picture, that we involve everyone from the beginning, that we are training, and that we are helping each other to deliver.

When we prepare to take our following step and I ask my team what will be crucial for success, they will say:

"We are going to create the best picture, to really make sure everyone is involved from the beginning, that we are following our time table, and that we will take the best help that we can find because we are going to deliver with brilliance."

Our Co-workers will Grow with Our Movement

Each co-worker will take on complementary responsibilities to make sure that we will build up our new strong supporting culture. Our documentation will give a deeper understanding about, and involvement in, how we can be more professional together. Step-by-step we will build up our possible future; we all have readiness inside.

Your reflections!

– Secure the proactive thoughts you now have in your mind to take your team towards the lead.

– Find out your approach regarding how to help your team get the best supportive Documentation for their movement.

MY FOUR MOST IMPORTANT

_____

_____

_____

_____

THIS IS HOW I WILL ORGANIZE WITH MY TEAM TO PROVIDE
OURSELVES WITH THE BEST DOCUMENTATION

THIS IS WHEN

THIS IS HOW WE WILL USE OUR DOCUMENTATION

WE MAKE OUR DOCUMENTATION CONSTRUCTIVE AND FUN

Part One:
The Basic Blocks

❏ Our Process

❏ Gather the Team

❏ Co-worker in the Center

❏ The We Spirit

❏ Documentation

Ask yourself, "Which parts will be most important for me to upgrade in order to strengthen my team?"

Part Two

Accelerating Our Movement

Accelerating Our Movement

You have now been through the first part of the K Concept.

Building up a strong, safe, and secure development process is the foundation for learning and progress.

Everyone on your team will be more connected and empowered by the upgrading of your team's common thinking process.

Everyone will end up with growing self-confidence because of your well-organized, professional leadership.

The more your co-workers are involved, the more they see and understand, the more they will be able to give into their unique part of the process, the better they can support others … and here we go!

Your more basic work will prepare your co-workers to further develop themselves. They will grow with your guiding leadership and now take their part of the business further, driving their contributions towards your ambitions.

You and your team will be ready to develop what you will call "the best way for us."

- Gather the team. You will use this way of working as a natural tool regularly and in needed situations.

In your plan for the year you will establish a rhythm for:

- Co-worker in the center meetings
- "We spirit" activities
- How and when you do your Documentation

You will find out how to efficiently outline your way of working together with your team.

The upcoming blocks will now support your ambitions to:

- Accelerate your team
- Accelerate your co-workers
- Give your contribution to your company's movement into the market of tomorrow

You will reflect on and grow your understanding about:

- Your role as an Engine in your company
- Being a leader in the Intelligent Company of your business

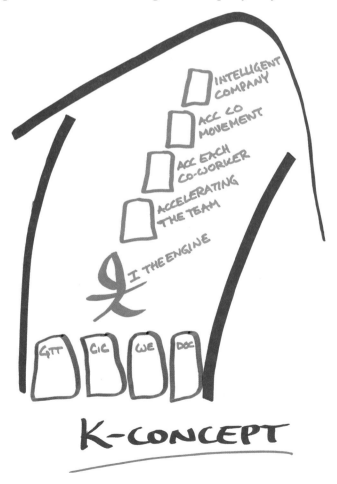

I, THE ENGINE

BOSS

NET

COLLEAGUES

TEAM

I GIVE MYSELF TIME TO THINK AND REFLECT
ABOUT MY CRUCIAL CONNECTIONS AND MYSELF

6

I, the Engine

You are the proactive leader in your niche.

Your openness will add new insights, and your training will add new skills. You will learn how to use your potential and resources to find "the best way for you," telling yourself:

I Am the Engine

I am an important engine in my company's business development.

I have the responsibility to lead my part of the business and I will work hard to connect my team, my colleagues, and the leaders I report to with the edge of our market.

My Team

I will regularly gather my team to discuss our situation and our opportunities, making sure that we have the right co-worker in every crucial position, and that we are building up the best strategic connections and support to be an outstanding partner of our value stream.

My Leadership Team

The leadership team I belong to is of course a crucial key to our company's progress, and I will work hard to make sure that we

I, the Engine

are cooperating efficiently when connecting our unique parts of the business.

We will work on our common picture by taking guidance from our overall company picture, coordinating information, processes, and people. The better connected we all are in the leadership team, the more we will be able to bring clarity in our own teams and tie our business together towards customer appreciation.

My Boss

It is crucial to me that my boss and I dig deeper to find common ground in our ideas. I will give information, ideas, and insights from my part of the business and my boss will connect with strategic guidance from the executive team and their points of view.

The more of the big picture, constructive ideas, and energy I receive from my boss, the more contribution I will be able to create with my part of the business.

We Develop a Strong Infrastructure

To be the great leader—the Engine—it is important to be part of a strong leadership infrastructure like the one described. Sometimes it is valuable to bring in extra coaching and mentoring from outside specialists for guidance and additional support to achieve the best possible overview, strategy, programs, and tools for how to move things forward in the short- and long-term perspectives.

Your reflections!

– Secure your thoughts on the following page:

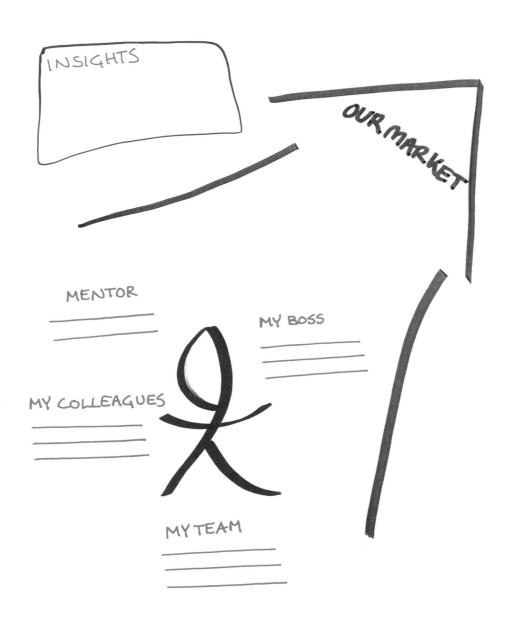

INSIGHTS

OUR MARKET

MENTOR
_____
_____

MY BOSS
_____
_____
_____

MY COLLEAGUES
_____
_____
_____

MY TEAM
_____
_____
_____

BUILDING MYSELF STRONGER
FILL IN MOST IMPORTANT ACTIONS

To Be Strong in Your Role as Leader

Your openness will add new insights, and your training will add new skills. You will learn how to use your potential and resources to find "the best way for you."

We Are Inventing Our Lives and Roles as We Live

It is challenging to be the Engine. It is a lot about connecting, balancing, and sometimes politics.

Some leaders understand better than others how to take care of themselves, their family, and friends to create a healthy distance from their work role in order to relax and just enjoy life.

Since we are inventing our lives and roles as we live, it is important that we are connected to the guidelines in our society, our surrounding culture. Staying connected to guidelines and culture happens when we are open to influences from family, friends, and selected key people.

We Support Each Other

The better I understand our social pattern to support each other, I will recognize how people are trying to support me to take care of my body, mind, and spirit. They want me to work out, to know about nutrition, to develop relationships, as well as be successful in my profession.

I want to support them.

We support each other to understand life from birth until 100— all our different ages. We support each other to understand our different stages in life, empowering each other to take each next step by releasing more of our unique individual potential with positive and constructive minds. After taking a step, we support each other to understand ourselves in the new situation.

We Develop Insights and Make New Choices

We discuss the meaning of life and how much people are willing to contribute when building up something new, bigger, and better. We discuss how it can be possible to reflect this back to people so that everyone can feel proud and satisfied with their accomplishments.

- How can we act more grateful?
- How can we all be stronger in living our values?

There are so many interesting questions and thoughts that will grow our perspectives as leaders, as we give ourselves time for thinking, upgrading, and training to renew ourselves. Our experiences will grow into insights so we will make important next choices that will release fresh motivation and energy to train and to act new, in a more powerful way.

Life Is a Journey

Life is a journey; our family situation will develop into coming steps. We will meet new friends, new key people, meet upcoming ages and new stages in our profession, and we will view meaning and values from more experienced perspectives.

We Are Leading the Movement

The better we realize our situation, the stronger Engines we will become. We have our unique leadership gift and we have developed skills to support people to connect and be part of the movement.

I, the Engine

We support people to better recognize their situation, empowering them to connect and commit to the new, bigger, and better. As leaders we support people to leave, to forgive, to forget, and to move on.

With the belief that good news is coming, they will prepare to capture the opportunities they will be given.

Your reflections!

– Secure your important thoughts about building yourself stronger on the following page:

INSIGHTS

VALUES IMPORTANT FOR ME

ROUTINES TO UPGRADE

MY FRIENDS

HOW WE REFLECT ON LIFE AND SUPPORT EACH OTHER

MY STRONG ROUTINES

BUILDING MYSELF STRONGER
FILL IN MOST IMPORTANT ACTIONS

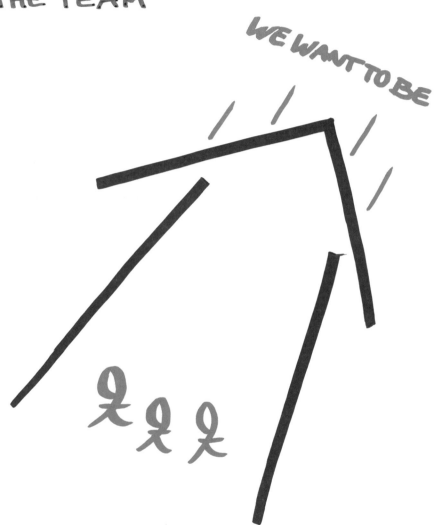

ACCELERATING
THE TEAM

WE WANT TO BE

CONNECTING OUR COWORKERS INTO OUR FUTURE

7

Accelerating the Team

Accelerate your team's movement towards the edge of your market.

Speeding Up

Up until now we have been developing a strong and secure team. When we have this basic trust in our team, people are ready to speed up our movement.

The mental creation comes first and as leaders we have to intensify our work of connecting our co-workers' hearts and minds into the future, into visions and choices about "who we want to be." Our decisions will guide us in what to do and our choices will fill us with determination and release energy to go for it.

This is how I unite my team to take our next step:

Our Strengths

I will ask everyone to draw the picture you can see on the next page, and then write down his or her individual view about our team's strengths today.

- Externally—our position relative to the market edge
- Internally—the core behind our business

Our "Want To Be" Pictures

Secondly, I inspire everyone to draw his or her "want to be" picture describing us two to three years from now, or at the end of our project.

Our Key Factors

Thirdly, I empower everyone to figure out and write down the four most important factors that will take us from where we are today to where we want to be tomorrow.

Our Common Ideas

When everyone has his or her picture ready, we will divide into groups of four or five and ask each member of the group to really listen to each other, take notes, reflect, then discuss, and come up with the picture for the whole group.

When the groups have their contributions ready, we will come together and first listen carefully to each other, take notes, and reflect further.

This following discussion can show how important we think it is to know and understand:

- Our company history, our core, and our soul
- How crucial it is to be united around our direction

Reflections will make us aware of how our pictures complement each other and how several of our key factors are the same.

Our Consensus

I will highlight the **consensus** we have about our movement and underline that the starting point in every discussion is what we are united around.

Of course, several of the key factors in the individual pictures are different, which is the way it should be.

We are different individuals with different knowledge, experiences, insights, and expectations. All of the identified factors will probably be important in the long run. It is crucial for us at this point to clarify what we all can agree on so we can start to act and accelerate together.

We are always part of something bigger

With all the inputs from our team I am now responsible for developing our unique picture. During this process I will involve my boss and selected key people to ensure that the picture will be as clear as possible and in line with our overall company vision and business strategies. After meeting with my bosses, I will gather my team to bring further clarity about our possible ambitions and polish our common picture even further. It is crucial that we are all behind our important picture—that is what business is all about, common agreement on how to create value.

We look for our contributions

My role is now to connect the overall picture down to the individual co-worker with his or her part of the business, and to make sure that all our ambitions will be in line. Since everyone is already connected and understands the ambition of our strategy, these will be creative meetings. We organize our overall ambitions into lots of smaller steps. We may apply various natural steps, like time frames of half a year or by planning certain steps of a project.

- If the overall key factor is to develop unique market-knowledge, the co-worker's goal may be to develop more knowledge about our customers and competitors during the coming months.
- If the overall key factor is to develop a technological edge, during the next months or the next step of our project the goal can be to develop our IT skills.

We want it to be well-organized

We organize in steps.

The key is to involve every co-worker to be the driver of our ambitions, strengthening our learning development process. Every co-worker has ideas regarding what we want to know more about in each area. For example, our customer.

We discuss and decide on each co-worker's initiatives and we go out to gather information to bring back to the team. Everyone will now have crucial inputs to share with the team so that they can easily give 3 to 5-minute presentations. Within an hour we will have lots of substantial information on our table.

We will go through every main area in this fashion: after sharing our new information we will every time generate a broader and deeper picture which will feed our involvement and movement.

We are cooperating in an efficient, well-organized way.

We generate strategic intelligence

Our well-organized cooperation will generate strategic intelligence to drive our business. Cooperation skills will increase dramatically inside our team and together with all parts of our value-stream, as well as other important individuals and teams.

We move towards the step of option

Our well-organized movement will guide us toward the market edge through the "step of option." We are approaching the "step of option" because the team is growing and developing. The team is developing because the individuals are developing. We need strong individuals with strong confidence who can find out about new initiatives and take on new responsibilities so we can create our unique way of how to move forward—to **live** our vision.

Living Our Vision

By living our vision, we are interacting in a fresh way with our surroundings. We develop new guiding pictures, we reflect, and we discuss information while trying to be more proactive, with the ambition to use more of our brainpower resources. We connect ourselves to new sources looking for technological drivers and trends in the market.

We are communicating in new ways.

We are transforming our team, guided by higher values, trying to be more professional and proactive in every area.

Your reflections!

– Secure what you find as most important when accelerating towards your ambitions.

– Follow the template, rate your actual situation, and make conclusions about actions to accelerate your movement.

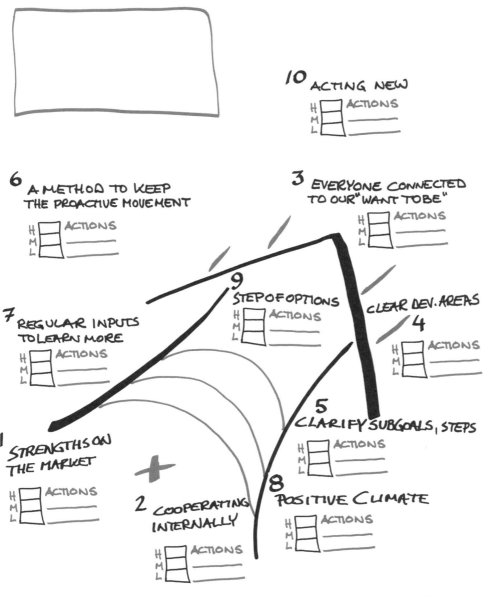

10 ACTING NEW

H M L ACTIONS

6 A METHOD TO KEEP
THE PROACTIVE MOVEMENT

H M L ACTIONS

3 EVERYONE CONNECTED
TO OUR "WANT TO BE"

H M L ACTIONS

9 STEP OF OPTIONS

H M L ACTIONS

CLEAR DEV. AREAS

4

H M L ACTIONS

7 REGULAR INPUTS
TO LEARN MORE

H M L ACTIONS

1 STRENGTHS ON
THE MARKET

H M L ACTIONS

2 COOPERATING
INTERNALLY

H M L ACTIONS

5 CLARIFY SUBGOALS, STEPS

H M L ACTIONS

8 POSITIVE CLIMATE

H M L ACTIONS

RATING OUR DEVELOPMENT - HIGH, MEDIUM, LOW -
WILL EMPOWER US TO FIND MOST IMPORTANT ACTIONS

ACCELERATING EACH COWORKER

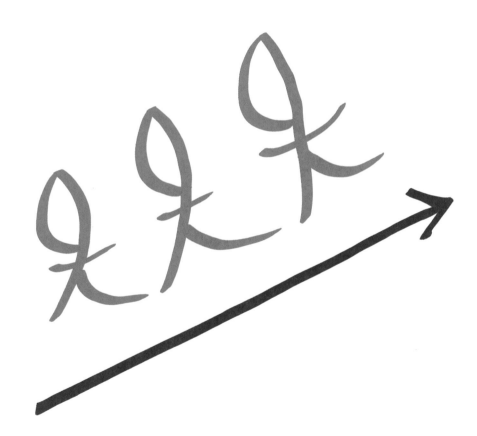

INVESTING IN EACH OTHER'S DEVELOPMENT

8

Accelerating Each Co-worker

Grow your co-workers to accelerate your development.

A Solid Team

When we enroll our children in their first sports team, we want it to be a solid team. When the children begin school, we want them to be in a solid class. When they are growing up and start their professional work, we want them to be a part of a solid team in a solid company.

When you ask parents what they mean by this, they normally say, "We want to create the best opportunities for our children so they can release their full potential and live out their vision. Our children, therefore, need the best education and training." Then they usually add, "But life is so much more."

- We want our children to learn about the world that they are a part of, and develop their intellectual intelligence.
- We want them to learn how to handle different situations, the ups and downs, developing their emotional intelligence.

- We want them to be part of a culture where they see themselves as strong and safe while learning to develop and keep the best relationships, developing their social intelligence.
- We want them to stay fair and follow the law, rules, and agreements, developing their moral intelligence.

We want all of the above for our loved ones as much as we want and need it ourselves. As leaders, we want to create this environment for all our co-workers. The more we can develop our co-workers on all levels, the stronger and more proactive they will become.

Individual Coaching

I give individual coaching and organize support from outside sources for each co-worker on my team, to really support them. The more coaching I give each co-worker, the more he or she can release their potential. The better the quality of my coaching, the more my co-workers will release their potential.

In business we can coach before, during, and after, for example, a sales process or R&D process. We can give coaching in connection to unique meetings or presentations.

There is a lot to learn about coaching from the world of sports. Players are coached in long-term strategy and short-term tactics, such as before, during, and after a game or practice.

Coaching before a game can highlight:

- Readiness for what to expect from the other team
- How to fulfill our own tactics

- How to keep our energy and momentum
- How we stay fair and professional

Coaching before a practice can consist of:

- What to particularly focus on and why
- Whom to learn from
- How to keep and grow our constructive mindset

It is crucial to do the coaching step-by-step. While challenging, be realistic, for the co-worker to see and feel progress and momentum at each step. It is crucial to support the co-worker's awareness of that we are moving into new steps because of our decisions, training, and support.

How can I support my co-workers more?

It is very encouraging to see my co-workers growing. This will empower me to grow my leadership skills further, which also will build and grow my confidence.

My stronger confidence will make me more open, thus accelerating our dialogue:

- How can I support you even more?
- What are your expectations of me?
- Their answer will be: be there when we need you.

When I ask my team for more specific answers, they will say:

- Support us, as you usually say, with body, mind, and spirit
- Make sure we are connected with the future
- Drive us to develop our skills to be the best we can be
- Be there when we are facing new risks and issues

After listening to their expectations, I will ask, "What can I expect from you?"

- That we are developing individually as much as we can and continue to be a team player in the same person.
- That we will develop strong relationships within our team and with crucial outside sources.
- That we always think about quality in every meeting and every endeavor, looking for guidance from the edge of our market.

An Example from Sports

I will give an example from the world of sports to illustrate some opportunities when creating a solid team.

I am the leader and one of my hockey players wants to improve his shooting skills.

- He tries to score close to the post, but he shoots wide. He tells himself, "Next time I will score."
- Next time he shoots wide again, and he tells himself, "Next time I must score!"
- He shoots wide a third time. Now his self-confidence has eroded and he starts to tell himself, "I can't!"

With that in mind he of course shoots wide again and this time he tells himself, "I am worthless!"

The Picture

As the leader my role is to keep my player out of this emotional mess and I can easily do that by supporting him with energy: "Come on, you have all the qualities that it takes to score!"

I also support my player with constructive ideas: "If you start a little bit closer to the goal and work from that ..."

I take charge to keep the player connected with the only thing that can help him or her—the mental picture of successfully scoring.

Our Inner Dialogue

We always have our inner dialogue going on. On the lowest level of this inner dialogue we are telling ourselves, "I can't, we have no energy." No guiding picture.

On the next level we tell ourselves, "I must succeed." Now we are building up energy, but our guiding picture is blurry. We used to end up frustrated.

As a solid leader I bring my player up to the next level by helping him connect to his overall "want to be picture" to release energy, then we make his supporting picture of the situation crystal clear so the player starts to release his energy and his self-confidence. I do it like this:

I support my player to refresh and polish the guiding picture so it becomes as helpful as it needs to be. When these pieces are in place, the player has to practise and polish to move to his desired level. I can do this!

We All Need Upgraded Pictures

Wherever we are in life, we will benefit from a better supporting picture, the picture that can help us reach our expectations.

There are so many alternatives to support ourselves with a better picture. The key is to take help from other people, leaders, co-workers, mentors, and so on. Sometimes we need several pictures at the same time to support our inner ambition. We create long-term, short-term, and "now" perspectives for stabilization, and for the emergence of our winning picture. To reach success there is always added focused training.

I Am a Picture Builder

My role as a leader is to make sure that all my co-workers or players have this winning picture fresh in their minds.

I am responsible for the picture building process in our team— I am a picture builder.

Our Supportive Culture

Creating a supportive culture is a challenge. In the beginning when the player was practicing, his teammates were laughing when he was shooting wide; this will bring the player down.

In creating a supportive culture, we need education, and we stress that to become the champions that we decided to be, our opportunity is that everyone will be successful through all our training. We develop our understanding of building a culture where we all support each other with energy and constructive ideas.

Our common vision supports us to cooperate

It takes strong leadership to create a solid team. Being a strong leader, I connect my players into our common vision, into our steps, into our agreements. Once connected, the older player will listen to the younger player's new ideas and take in his energy. The younger player will listen to the older player's experiences and try to learn from their skills. Our common vision will keep our minds open to desired progress.

We will be the champions

When our players and co-workers feel that they are an important part of what we want to accomplish, they will start to believe in what they are doing and support each other's development and self-renewal.

We are going to become the champions we decided on being, because in this supportive climate amazing things will happen.

Your reflections!

- First, secure your reflections on the following page.

- Second:
  a) fill in the template with key words and images to get your own guidance.
  b) reflect on how you will use the template when supporting your co-workers.

- Third, go through "The Winner Strategy" concept on pages 110–111. Find out how you can create a coaching discussion that will support your co-worker to better understand how to grow as part of your team in your market situation.

- Ask questions and take notes, discuss, then draw and write together. Start with your easier co-workers. This will, step-by-step, give you needed training and progress.

I'm the picture builder!

The right balance between the co-workers' pictures will release their development, their inner ambition, their drive.

The following pages will give you a basic concept for next level coaching to further accelerate your co-worker's development.

"THE WINNER STRATEGY"

Ask for background   earlier work, ambition...

Ask for possible
contributions   want to be,
self-picture...

Discuss company big
picture and roles  to better understand
himself in the business

Strengthen positive
inner dialogue   4 3 **PICTURE** 2 1   find the best
supportive picture,
then train

Strengthen positive
relationships in every
direction      to be free

Discuss being unique and a team player at the same time

I make the team strong, my team makes me strong

Discuss how the habit of "being prepared" will make you free to be the best you can be

to go for it

Find out how to support positive outer dialogue

to take responsibility and affect our movement

Make clear who to learn from

to grow awareness and find role models

Make clear the importance of staying behind common agreements

always put on the table and solve inside the team

Accelerating our Company Movement

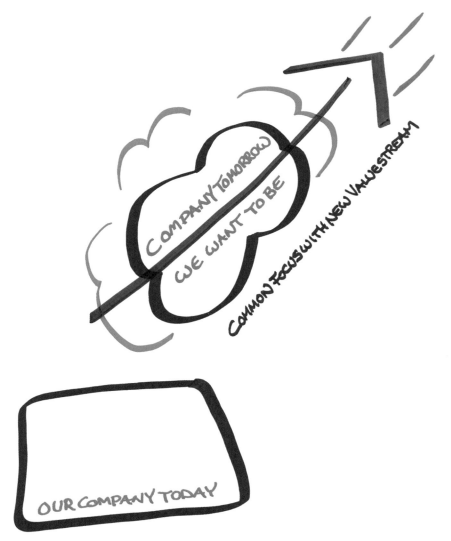

Company Tomorrow We Want To Be

Common Focus with New Valuestream

Our Company Today

Connecting our Organization into our Future Estimated Value

9

Accelerating Our Company Movement

Lead your team into tomorrow as the proactive part of your company.

Accelerating Our Company Movement

So far we have been working with determination to develop our teams and our co-workers. Some parts of our business are more successful while other parts are struggling.

The Technological Drive

We are only one player in the huge development where companies all the time are looking for new ways to catch the market's attention.

Technology is a main driver to success as we talk about overview, communication, logistics codes, images, and lots of new spaces.

Companies that are specialists in communication, logistics, and entertainment industries are often seen as the frontiers.

Our Global Environment

The global environment will challenge us to accelerate our movement towards our new paradigm. The energy and CO_2 situation will empower all of us to be more efficient, to find new sources, and to behave in new ways.

- How can we lift our company to meet all new opportunities?
- How can my company become an important part in creating new value from scarce resources, meeting global expectations of sustainability?

The end customers' voices will give demanding guidance.

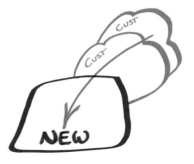

Our Current Situation

Looking into the current situation of our company, we are creating market pull from our customers' second interface and their market situation. We are bringing our troops together, supporting them to be more efficient, more lean, at the same time we are developing "the new" applications, services, and solutions.

We are in a situation where external demands and internal ambitions sometimes have competing focuses. In connection with the quarterly results, we can easily be trapped into a shortsighted mindset.

Our New Paradigm

Looking towards tomorrow, we are searching for long term guidance. There will be lots of opportunities. It will be crucial to know "who we want to be."

The "want to be" discussion we have been through inside our teams will now be a general discussion all over our company, facilitated by the executive team and the trained and strong leaders.

We will provide every co-worker with an understanding of our possible future. Every discussion, every meeting, will step-by-step bring clarity to:

- The unique value we can bring to the future market
- Our thinking behind new strategic approaches
- The strengths we have in our company today

We will find out about new external cooperation with customers, suppliers, and other partners. We will unite around new internal cooperation, taking leadership of our movement.

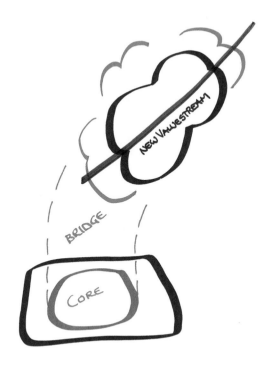

We are already moving

Because we have chosen to involve our people we are moving.

Our being will give us guidance to make our new priorities. We will find out about the core we have inside our company that can be the bridge into our future. We will polish and develop our core, find out what needs to be acquired to add value and what to leave behind, while creating new forms of support, growing into our new value stream.

Keywords in our new stream will be:

- INTEGRATE
- SUPPORT
- SPECIALIZE
- LEAD

We will:

- Integrate our departments into the next level of cooperation.
- Build deeper connections and common strategies with selected customers in the new global market using our common insights of how the new global situation will develop.
- Build deeper connections and common strategies with our selected suppliers in the new global market and the same with our partners, guided by our future opportunities.

We will develop common pictures together with our new selected value stream. This will help us bring guidance on how to support and help each other with branding coverage, sales, after-market sales, R&D, IT—this will help us bring each other towards synergies. These synergies will allow each part of the new value stream to give more focus to their unique contributions. Together we will take the lead in our market.

We will listen carefully to each other to find out how we can build trust in the future market, how we can find "our unique way."

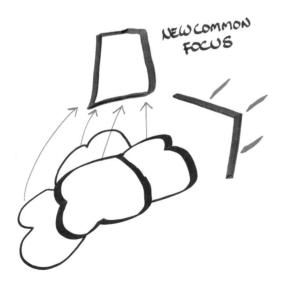

We know a lot about well-organized development

The good thing is that we know a lot about the movement. We know how to create stability and trust through gathering teams, putting the co-worker in the center, and developing we spirit and cohesion. Through documentation we reflect our movement from the outside in.

We know how to build strong teams and how to grow co-workers and key people, so we will be like the engine in our stream's development.

Empowering and guiding our partners, we lift our value stream towards long-term success.

We are guided by our new common focus.

Your reflections!

– Secure your thoughts about how to lead your company into tomorrow. Fill out the template on the following page:

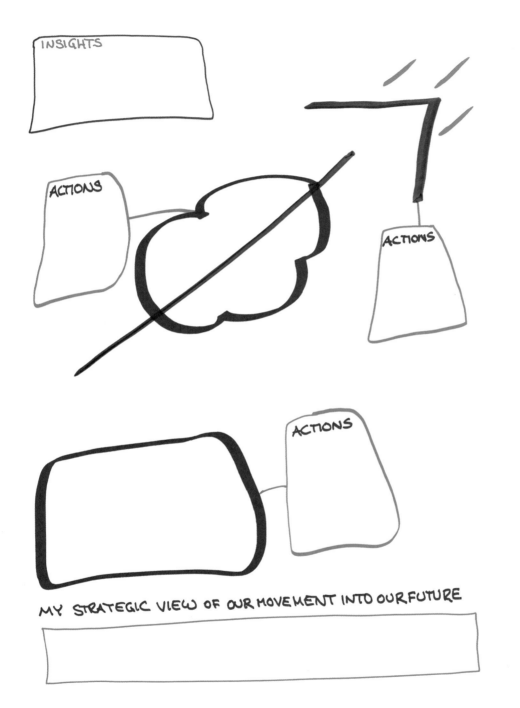

INTELLIGENT COMPANY

New World

NEW INDIVIDUAL RESPONSIBILITY

NEW COMMON RESPONSIBILITY

VALUES

THE BEST WAY FOR US!

10

Intelligent Company

Our Intelligent Company will move with high speed in the new market, guided by deep understanding of and strong commitment to "who we want to be."

The Best Way for Us

How do we find the best way for us?

How do we find a solid path where we have the foresight to lead the value-generating process that we are responsible for?

How can we be the intelligent company?

These are the main questions for each executive team and for each leader.

We know it's a blend of a lot, where the success comes out of the executive team's skills to organize and lead on several levels simultaneously, connecting people's ambitions towards a common focus. It is to establish a company culture with a proactive connecting mindset. It is about creating the logistics for continuous involvement of everyone for the long-term perspective.

We are developing the new world through a positive mindset about our future, helping us explore opportunities that will connect to our dreams and empower us to act new.

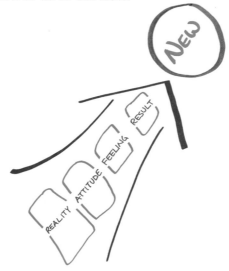

Our Basic Picture

The results we get are affected by a feeling we have about the actual situation.

Our feeling comes out of our attitudes. For example, if it starts snowing during a football game, we may lose focus and energy because we have an old mindset that football should be played in decent weather. In reality football is played in sun, in rain, in snow. My role as a leader is to support my players to realize this so we will be motivated to develop our skills to handle every situation. I will further support my players to learn about the teams we are going to play, their strengths, their key players, and their tactics.

There is so much preparation we can easily do, from the start of the game all the way to how to perform when there is five minutes left and we are ahead, if we are even, or if we are under—these are our tactics.

Before each game we will evaluate and ask each other: what is the situation?

We will make our decision of how to approach the game. Our common decision will support each player to make the best individual decision about "my best contribution," ensuring that each one will be as proactive as possible to reach their best performance.

The Same Mind in Business

It's the same scenario in business. The results we get are affected by our feelings about the situation, which come out of our attitude. We go with old products into new markets, we take new products into old markets, and sometimes we go with new products into new markets.

As a leader I have a lot of work to do with my co-workers to upgrade our understanding so we will be motivated to develop competencies and tactics. We will learn about different markets and different companies and unite ourselves in our strategic business approach.

In preparing a meeting, we will ask each other: what is the situation? We will support the team to develop clarity, and to be united in our common ambition. Our decision will give guidance to each involved co-worker to make his or her individual decision about their best contribution. We want everyone to be as proactive as possible to reach the best common result.

With Fresh Minds People Cooperate in New Ways

We are developing the new world when acting in new interesting ways. We take on new joint and individual responsibilities to establish a culture with a proactive connecting mindset that is guided by overall agreed-upon values.

The Executive Team Develops the Core

In the intelligent company the executive team understands that it is important to take on leadership. They work hard to be "the strong core" that will lead the company movement.

The executive team provides the organization with the important overall strategic direction, giving guidance to all ambitions that exist inside their company and co-workers. Executives guide out of broader time frames like spring—fall—spring—fall.

The executive team takes individual and joint responsibility to help where help is needed in the organization and act with energy and constructive ideas to move things forward. Their responsibility is to every day make the value stream more efficient.

The executive team supports all the leaders in the organization to take the next step in developing their part of the business. They do it through personal interaction and through programs.

Each Co-worker's Contribution Makes a Difference

The executive team understands individual and joint responsibility, so that all of the co-workers will upgrade their understanding and be motivated to develop their skills and desires. Executives understand that the key is to involve them in tactics and the decision-making process.

The executive team expects each co-worker to generate strategic intelligence in their niche with their part of the business.

Co-workers will bring up the best ideas in their teams, go after the best in the value stream, look for the market edge, and go to the leaders for guidance and confirmation.

The Board's Contribution Will Make a Difference

It is crucial for the executive team to bring clarity in the organization about ambitions and guidelines from owners and board. It is crucial to regularly discuss with owners and board the organization's actual situation in the perspectives of long-term and short-term ambitions. Developing deeper understanding and more involvement between all players in the movement is the ultimate key in every solid business development. This will lead to the next step of committed choices, moving the business forward.

The leaders in the executive team take individual and joint responsibility for the quality of the communication to bring all shareholders into understanding and clarity of how to be sponsors of their company's unique development. How can they all give their best contribution, building this value-generating corporation?

Your reflections!

– Secure your picture of the intellient company below.

INSIGHTS

ACTIONS – EX LEAD TEAM

ACTIONS – FOR ME   ACTIONS – EACH LEADER

Part Two:
The Accelerating Blocks

❏ I, the Engine

❏ Accelerating the Team

❏ Accelerating Each Co-worker

❏ Accelerating Our Company Movement

❏ Intelligent Company

Write down the parts that you find most important for you leading your team towards the market edge.

Part Three

Building Our "Tomorrow"

Building Our Tomorrow Takes Architecture and Consistency

As we create our well-organized development, we now see as important:

- Broadening every co-worker's big picture about our business and the market.
- Intensifying the development in each part of the process within the company.
- Implementing a method supporting basic communication inside and between each part of our company.
- Building up driving forces for technological and human development support, for people and processes.

Moving forward, people first want to see and think about how to act new.

They will then try a little bit, think further, and finally they start to do focused training, trying new steps to act more proactive.

It will take consistency to keep up the direction through accelerating understanding and involvement, so choices will be made and upcoming results will give momentum.

The movement is a learning development process, and we provide our organization with programs and logistics to grow towards decided steps.

This is important to understand that our history is a culture of telling; someone told you, managed you. We moved into more of working in teams, helping each other find direction from the customer's expectations. We are now in a global economy where it's about giving guidance to the market. We connect ourselves through the latest technology with lots of new options. We connect with other driving proactive players.

In our group of people a few will be able to intellectually understand new more efficient ways of cooperating and at the same time have confidence and will power to take action. They will go first. Others will need their guidance. They are developing themselves more out of social coping; they start to follow when they see others progress. Still others will demand more guidance, training, and support or find new positions. We support each other to always remember, we work out of this reality.

Connecting and growing the leaders we have in our company, we know what they are looking for so we:

- Develop more mentorship in our organization.
- Give more support to leaders to grow in their current roles so they can take on new interesting processes.
- Support them to connect to networks that give what they are really looking for.
- Support them to find and build up the core of people together with whom they can make a difference.

Our overall goal is to support them, to generate energy, intelligence, skills, and tactics to accelerate and create great results with their teams.

The executive team has to keep fresh in mind how they can make a difference from their position:

- Support, so more and more people in the organization start to connect into proactive thinking about the realistic future. With this mindset, co-workers start to see opportunities and soon they will start to act new.

- Understanding how statements committing to people's higher values and the deeper understanding we have inside, will be essential.
- Show they understand that their co-workers are expecting the leaders in the company to guarantee the infrastructure that will put them into new steps of learning and development, so they will raise their value compared to the market edge.

The key to every development is having the mindset of helping each other and understanding the importance of being united around how and when to take help from outside sources.

The top team's skill at establishing this mindset throughout the company will accelerate the growth of individuals, teams, and results.

Helping complementary groups, departments, and units openly find out and communicate how they can give their best support to each other, and also to express which help they need from each other, is the biggest growth potential in many organizations.

Great leadership at the top will connect ambitions of progress into company excellence.

The CEO's and the executive team's understanding and skills will make the difference when sketching our future and when moving into tomorrow.

Moving Into Tomorrow

I have over the years been involved in several development processes. I have recognized the happiness and excitement in the eyes of people when they get the chance to give their best contributions, sensing that their input gives meaningfulness, respect, and results.

This gives an empowering dimension to our important leadership role.

To further support your thinking process I will highlight what I see as three important challenges that will give lots of meaningfulness and respect to determined leaders in the coming years.

Guiding our technological development
Guidance into our green future
To leave our legacy

Taking leadership and creating our future, we one way or another engage in these areas.

The more I involve myself, the more I will be involved …

It's so empowering to have really interesting concerns to grow with; this situation will force me to connect myself with others. Looking for other people and processes with the same important ambition will keep me alert, alive, and young in mind.

In the following inputs, you will read about some interesting people and their processes, to inspire yourself about tomorrow.

GUIDING OUR TECHNOLOGICAL DEVELOPMENT

11
Guiding Our Technological Development

SLW is a U.S. law firm specializing in intellectual property law, serving such clients as E-bay, Adobe, Intel, and several universities. In the fifteen years since it was founded, the firm has gained a national reputation for its high-quality patent work, ranked number one in overall patent quality by Ratings LLC for three consecutive years.

SLW offers a full range of expertise, including software, mechanical, pharmaceutical chemistry, biotechnology, electrical engineering, semiconductor, and medical devices.

Steve Lundberg is the president and founding partner of the firm headquartered in Minneapolis. He is an entrepreneurial leader and a master of creating interest among his people in how to move forward. The core of the SLW business is to help their clients capture their new technological advancements in forms of patents and other intellectual property, to further develop their markets, and SLW wants to be an active force in this movement.

SLW has established its mindset by continuously generating ideas with customers, co-workers, specialists, and so on. Steve and his team have been the engine, creating a well-organized development for productivity and pro-activity, inspiring:

- New ways of acting
- New support tools
- Lots of next steps

Below is one example of a concept, showing how the firm is trying to be this unique force in finding and securing the technological development to support their clients. It started as an ambition to support clients to better manage their patent portfolios.

Better Manage Your Patent Portfolio

The first step is to help their clients, or give support to other patent experts with their clients, to rapidly sort, rank, and analyze patents.

One part of a patent is the description of the invention, called the specification. The other part is called the claim and describes the limited area where the patent gives the patent holder the rights to exclude others from practicing the invention during the patent's term.

To get an overview of a mid-size patent portfolio of, let's say, 500 patents with 2,000 independent claims, the so-called mining and mapping process used to take five-to-twenty-five attorney days of manual labor.

Envision a device that would present a panoramic view of your company's patent claims and even patent claims for applications within one or more technology areas. Patents presented side-by-side, in detail, showing all claims and what those claims cover.

Envision that the same could be done with your competitors' patent claims, printed on a map that you can put on the meeting table, easily understood by your whole team.

Envision this, after some time, done in fifteen-to-twenty minutes instead of the five to twenty-five attorney days.

Steve and his team have been working on this for years. Together, with technology specialists, they have now launched their supporting concept in a form of more than 200 client maps, generating a visibility into patent claim coverage that previously has been unattainable. The firm has accelerated itself into the "step of option."

This claim mapping concept does require substantial work up-front by skilled patent lawyers; this is what SLW and other law firms are recognized for. Once the patents are entered and categorized and the software data is ready to analyze, the output is incredibly accurate and comes in record time, giving lawyers and clients more time to do the crucial strategic work.

The overview will give growing clarity about actual strengths, as well as guidance towards white space areas for the next step of development.

This is the second step of the concept where the firm is able to better connect the best available support they can give, to the clients' growing clarity about their opportunities to move forward.

The improved overview is now the driver in the technological development, letting every company get their arms around their own situation regarding patent protection and opportunities.

They become able to make lots of important strategic decisions out of their core.

My consultants and I have been one of the proactive forces SLW has been using to take their business towards this new paradigm. We have been their outside support, strengthening their common ground for new decisions and initiatives.

When taking the next step of development with every organization we know, we connect every co-worker into their common picture of tomorrow and the path there, with needed symbolic convergence about the movement. It's amazing how common pictures will take us into tomorrow.

Below you have examples of some broader pictures which can be helpful in every development.

BUILDING US STRONGER

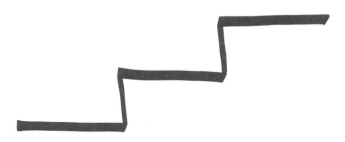

WE KNOW THAT LIFE IS A STEP-BY-STEP LEARNING DEVELOPMENT PROCESS
EACH STEP NEEDS TIME FOR THINKING, TRAINING AND PROGRESS
TOGETHER WE TAKE THE NEXT STEP

WE TAKE THE BEST, ADD, PRIORITIZE AND GO FOR IT

WE DEVELOP

WANT TO BE
STRATEGIC OVERVIEW
RIGHT PEOPLE
LEADERS
ALL LEADERSHIP
STRONG TEAMS
TOOLS
COMMUNICATION
WITH MARKET EDGE

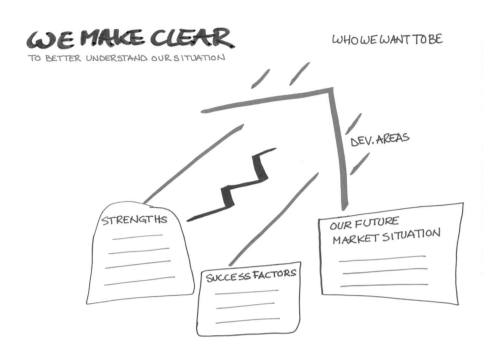

WE MAKE CLEAR
TO BETTER UNDERSTAND OUR SITUATION

WHO WE WANT TO BE

DEV. AREAS

STRENGTHS

SUCCESS FACTORS

OUR FUTURE MARKET SITUATION

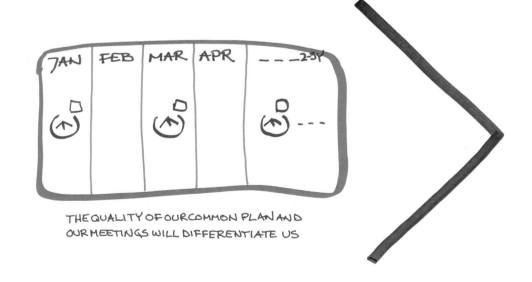

JAN	FEB	MAR	APR	— — —23Y

THE QUALITY OF OUR COMMON PLAN AND
OUR MEETINGS WILL DIFFERENTIATE US

OUR TECHNOLOGICAL DEVELOPMENT

THE MOST IMPORTANT TECH DEVELOPMENT
IN MY BUSINESS NEXT 2-3 Y.

MY STRENGTHS AS DRIVER

MY BEST HELP TO DRIVE THE DEVELOPMENT

IMPORTANT PICTURES SUPPORTING OUR MOVEMENT

GUIDANCE INTO OUR GREEN FUTURE

12
Guidance Into Our Green Future

The former U.S. ambassador in Sweden, Michael Wood, was doing important work extracting and highlighting Swedish start-up companies of interest when establishing our new green world.

His work was very important because his interest in future opportunities inspired Swedish politicians as well as influential people back in the U.S.

Of course, he connected with Mats Leijon at the Uppsala University. Today, Mats is a professor, a business leader for several start-up companies, and a worldwide authority in the area of generating and transmitting electricity.

Mats envisions solutions that work in practive. He is brilliant at applying guiding equations and formulas.

My company and I supported him and other important development processes at ABB during the 1990s. Mats received lots of personal awards and ABB won Editor's Choice Award.

In the year 2000, Mats gathered a group of ten people to be the working board investigating the opportunity of generating energy from sea waves. I am on that board and the company name is Seabased.

Wave energy is a continuous renewable energy source and the global wave energy potential is big.

Lots of work has been done. Today everything is well on its way towards making the energy source we dreamed about economically feasible.

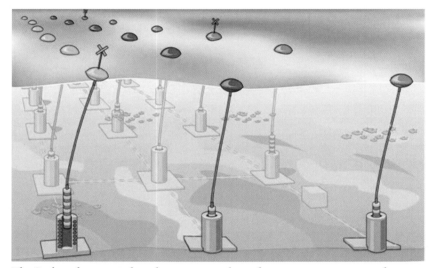

The Seabased system is based on a unique three-phase, permanent magnet, linear generator. It is developed to be deployed in ocean bed arrays and be directly driven by point absorbers on the surface.

The research team, in cooperation with Uppsala University, has done lots of basic work and has shown that this solution can generate electricity at low-wave amplitudes and relatively slow wave motions.

By deploying the generators in arrays on the ocean floor, a scalable power plant is achieved, which can extract substantial quantities of electric energy, even from milder ocean climate areas.

Seabased will be one example where commercial and environmental innovative energy technologies meet, and the green vision comes true.

There is an interesting world ahead of us—Our Green Future.

INTO OUR GREEN FUTURE

THIS IS MY VIEW OF OUR GREEN WORLD 2015
PICTURE + 5 KEYWORDS

THIS IS HOW I WILL BE INVOLVED IN CREATING
THIS NEW

THESE ARE PEOPLE AND PROCESSES I WILL
CONNECT TO, TO GIVE MY CONTRIBUTION

NAME	CONTRIBUTION
_____	_____
_____	_____
_____	_____

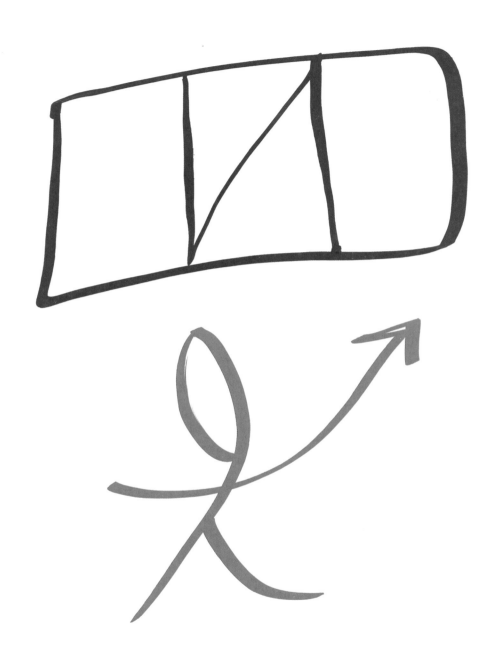

TO LEAVE OUR LEGACY

13

To Leave Our Legacy

Sometimes the thought of leaving a legacy, or simply just doing the right thing, might give birth to development. Making the world a better place is a demanding and pleasant task.

Percy Barnevik has been leading some of the world's biggest companies as CEO and/or chairman. Some such companies include ABB, AstraZeneca, Sandvik, and Skanska.

Some of the people we meet are extraordinary. They can be role models when moving minds over what's possible. Mr. Barnevik is one such role model.

He is now the chairman of and driver behind Hand in Hand International, a charity and support organization founded in 2006 that works with poor people in India, Afghanistan, South Africa, and other countries.

The ambition is to support people to get their arms around their own lives, as Mr. Barnevik describes it: "We are providing decentralized well-organized support; it's about giving people their option to take responsibility, and it's working!"

The focus of Hand in Hand is to alleviate rural poverty and empower women. Using a five-pillar program focusing on help to self-help, women first join groups and attend a 150-day crash course in literacy and numeracy. They are then trained in entrepreneurship, mentored, and offered micro loans to start businesses. To date more than 370,000 women have joined 25,000 self-help groups and over 100,000 businesses have started with an astonishing 99% success rate.

Alongside this program the charity works to free children from bonded labor, establishing transit schools for them. Medical camps are being set up in the villages along with citizen centers with libraries and IT facilities. Waste management and environmental projects are also put in place.

The Hand in Hand concept is run by strict commercial parameters with the view that elimination of poverty is the only way to peace.

Their enterprises range the gamut from catering, laundry, gardening, and manufacturing products such as toys.

Barnevik and the organization have pursued a vision of "mass-mobilization of the downtrodden people into entrepreneurship and economic growth." And this vision is coming true in virtually no time at all, proving that charity and business can go, no pun intended, hand in hand.

Hand in Hand is the best example imaginable of how to use managerial abilities and leadership skills to make a difference to our global village.

At this point it has employed about 4,000 co-workers, and there are 12,000 volunteers, many of whom have had important roles in Barnevik's prior organizations.

He probably has an open spot for all of his prior co-workers to show up and give their contribution, and the beauty of this story can inspire everyone.

Please take a look at www.hihseed.org for more information.

TO LEAVE OUR LEGACY

THIS IS THE LEGACY I WANT TO GIVE

THIS IS THE LEGACY I COULD GIVE FROM
AN OUTSIDE-IN PERSPECTIVE

THESE ARE PEOPLE AND PROCESSES I WILL
CONNECT TO, TO GIVE MY CONTRIBUTION

NAME	CONTRIBUTION
_____	_____
_____	_____
_____	_____

Part Four

Building
My Own Future

"I WANT TO BE"

14
I Want To Be!

Who do I want to be now?

Which perspectives do I take now?

How can I make a difference with my part of the business now?

How will my deeper connection with my future affect my perspectives now?

Moving towards my future ambition as leader, I have the same homework to do as my co-workers:

- First reflect on who I am and what took me here.
- Then polish the picture of my inner ambition and what I can be.
- Finally, find "the best way for me" to move there, in a well-organized way.

I am the architect of my future and I will find lots of support available for me to release even more of my potential when finding myself serving in a bigger context.

Now the final part of this book will challenge your thinking about "who you want to be."

Perspectives of My Journey as Leader

Looking back into my history, these are the key words describing my own strengths that have taken me here:

These are other strengths I possess:

This was my initial dream, being the leader.

How will my situation develop if I let one new big dream consume my mind?

This is the picture of what that dream can be:

To go for this dream I will first highlight what I already have:

Knowledge:

Insights:

Competencies:

Friends:

Connections:

More:

My reflection when looking at what I have built so far:

I Want To Be!

This is what I can easily add:

Knowledge:

Competencies:

Relationships:

Technology:

More:

My reflection when looking at what I can add:

I Will Discover More of Life

… because I am looking for the bright side …

Every new step has its unique path and life has always more to discover; that's the beauty of life.

I will discover that deciding to go for my new dream will lift my whole awareness into a new dimension and my body will respond with hunger, adrenaline, joy …

Fulfilling higher and deeper values will make us into what we are meant to be, so that we are driven towards new and more fruitful ways of acting.

… because I listen to my inner mission …

We say that we are driven by love. This love, what we feel deep inside, is our mission and contribution in life.

We make different choices to release our mission.

… because I support myself to make new choices …

I take time to think, listen, reflect, and train—this will build up my mind, skills, and desire to make the best choices.

I am unique—I show my strengths by being super at something.

I polish my core with the pictures of this something, then I train and develop further—I live it.

… because I upgrade my self-pictures …

This takes me to the question of the pictures I give to myself—which are my driving self-pictures, when acting as the leader.

Who do I want to be, how do I want to act?

Upgrading Your Guiding Self-Pictures

Below you have highlighted examples that can build you stronger when leading forward. You are the leader, the driving force, and your self-pictures will run your show. Please work through, digest, reflect, choose, add …

They are your pictures!

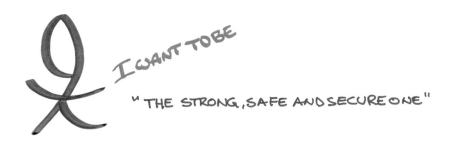

This is what I am particularly grateful about in life:

This is how I visualize myself acting grateful:

These are the strengths I feel in my working situation:

This is how I visualize myself— as being stronger in my working situation:

These are important relationships for me:

This is how I view myself developing my important relationships:

I WANT TO BE

" THE BIG ONE "

COOL CONSTRUCTIVE WHEN SITUATION

These are situations when I've been acting as "the big one":

This is how I want to see myself being "the big one":

I WANT TO BE

" THE CLEVER ONE "

LISTEN AND PUT INTO PERSPECTIVES

These are situations when I've been "the clever one":

This is how I would like to see myself being "the clever one":

"THE CARING ONE"

These are situations when I use to act as "the caring one":

This is how I want to act as "the loving caring one" in the future:

I WANT TO BE

GUIDING FROM HIGHER VALUES
GIVE STRENGTHS AND HOPE

These are situations when I've been guiding by higher values:

This is how I see myself acting, guiding by great values in the future:

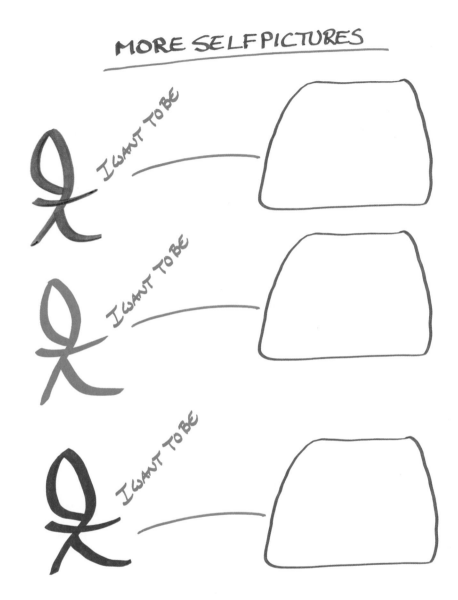

MORE SELF PICTURES

I WANT TO BE

I WANT TO BE

I WANT TO BE

Regularly connecting to my inner pictures will build up mental strengths, and I will grow myself as the leader.

I have a well inside waiting for me to explore, and I will find out how to guide and direct my inner dialogue.

I am the architect. I can repeat and visualize to myself every day that "I want to be ..."

- the Secure one
- the Loving one
- the Big one
- the Clever one
- Guiding from higher values
- And so on ...

So, here I am! and now and then it's natural that I will find myself reflecting on:

- Is my ambition to further develop my current situation?
- Maybe it's time to take my next step, to move on, challenged by my next exciting context, depending on where I am in life right now.

We are always on our way towards tomorrow—which brings happiness.

Acknowledgments

There are many people I want to thank for their help and support making this book come true, some of them are:

- Ellen Reid and her team for excellent book consulting and book production,

- everyone mentioned in the text; you all stand for strengths I admire,

- my network of consultants and friends for your important support and feedback,

- and to my wonderful family for your practical support and confidence in me. I appreciate you all very much.

KLINGBORG
UNDERSTANDING DEVELOPMENT

Contact us!

We provide:

♦ CEO support to coordinate and drive a well-organized strategic development in a large corporation.

♦ Speaking engagements to mobilize your people's movement into your future.

♦ Webinars to accelerate your co-worker's and team's development towards your strategy.

For contact information, please go to: www.leifklingborg.com

www.leifklingborg.com